Praise for Ilan Stavans

"Lively and intelligent, eclectic, sharp-tongued. . . ."
—PETER MATTHIESSEN

"Ilan Stavans has done as much as anyone alive to bridge the hemisphere's linguistic gaps."
—MIAMI HERALD

"Ilan Stavans is a maverick intellectual whose canonical work has already produced a whole array of marvels. . . . His incisive essays are redefining Jewish literature."
—FORWARD

"Our modern Antonio de Nebrija."
—ABC (SPAIN)

"Ilan Stavans is the rarest of North American writers—he sees the Americas whole. Not since Octavio Paz has Mexico given us an intellectual so able to violate borders, with learning and grace."
—RICHARD RODRIGUEZ

"In the multicultural rainbow that is contemporary America, no one may be more representative of the state of the union than Ilan Stavans."
—NEWSDAY

"Ilan Stavans may very well succeed in becoming the Octavio Paz of our age."
—SAN FRANCISCO CHRONICLE

"Ilan Stavans has the sharp eye of the internal exile. Writing about the sometimes reluctant reconquista of North America by Spanish-speaking cultures or the development of his own identity, he deals with both the life of the mind and the life of the streets."
—JOHN SAYLES

"An eagle-eyed critic whose oeuvre is a la par with that of George Steiner."
—JEWISH QUARTERLY

"Positive, exultant, anti-provincial, and inspiring, Stavans gives the reader the opportunity to celebrate the creation of a new Latino self in which we are not one but many, and the border becomes our 'dream catcher,' the magic web that permits us to reinvent the future."

—ROSARIO FERRÉ

"Stavans's work has opened the door to a better understanding of Hispanic culture in the United States."

—EL PAÍS (SPAIN)

"An erudite critic in the tradition of Octavio Paz and Edmund Wilson."

—NATION

"Stavans is an authentic polyglot and tricultural critic, editor and writer of numerous distinguished works."

—WASHINGTON POST

"Ilan Stavans is a disciple of Kafka and Borges. He accepts social identity broadly, in the most cosmopolitan terms. . . . His impulse is to broaden, not to narrow; he finds understanding through the complications of identity, not through the easy gestures of ethnic politics."

—NEW YORK TIMES

"Ilan Stavans, scholar, historian, polyglot, theoretician of two diasporas, is one of those rare intellectuals who seems willing to try his hand at anything."

—LOS ANGELES TIMES

The Oven

Also by Ilan Stavans

FICTION

The Disappearance

The One-Handed Pianist and Other Stories

NONFICTION

The Riddle of Cantinflas

Dictionary Days

On Borrowed Words

Spanglish

The Hispanic Condition

Art and Anger

Resurrecting Hebrew

A Critic's Journey

The Inveterate Dreamer

Octavio Paz: A Meditation

Imagining Columbus

Bandido

¡Lotería! (with Teresa Villegas)

José Vasconcelos: The Prophet of Race

Return to Centro Histórico

Singer's Typewriter and Mine

Gabriel García Márquez: The Early Years, 1929–1970

The United States of Mestizo

Reclaiming Travel (with Joshua Ellison)

Quixote: The Novel and the World

Borges, the Jew

I Love My Selfie (with Adál)

POETRY

The Wall

CONVERSATIONS

Knowledge and Censorship (with Verónica Albin)

What is la hispanidad? (with Iván Jaksić)

Ilan Stavans: Eight Conversations (with Neal Sokol)

With All Thine Heart (with Mordecai Drache)

Conversations with Ilan Stavans

Love and Language (with Verónica Albin)

¡Muy Pop! (with Frederick Aldama)

Thirteen Ways of Looking at Latino Art (with Jorge J. E. Gracia)

Laughing Matters (with Frederick Aldama)

CHILDREN'S BOOK

Golemito (with Teresa Villegas)

ANTHOLOGIES

The Norton Anthology of Latino Literature

Tropical Synagogues

The Oxford Book of Latin American Essays

The Schocken Book of Modern Sephardic Literature

Lengua Fresca (with Harold Augenbraum)

Wáchale!

The Scroll and the Cross
The Oxford Book of Jewish Stories
Mutual Impressions
Growing Up Latino (with Harold Augenbraum)
The FSG Book of Twentieth-Century Latin American Poetry
Oy, Caramba!

GRAPHIC NOVELS

Latino USA (with Lalo Alcaraz)
Mr. Spic Goes to Washington (with Roberto Weil)
Once @ 9:53 am (with Marcelo Brodsky)
El Iluminado (with Steve Sheinkin)
A Most Imperfect Union (with Lalo Alcaraz)
Angelitos (with Santiago Cohen)

TRANSLATIONS

Sentimental Songs, by Felipe Alfau
The Plain in Flames, by Juan Rulfo (with Harold Augenbraum)
The Underdogs, by Mariano Azuela (with Anna More)
Lazarillo de Tormes
El Little Príncipe, by Antoine de Saint Exupéry

EDITIONS

Cesar Vallejo: Spain, Take this Chalice from Me
The Poetry of Pablo Neruda
Encyclopedia Latina (4 volumes)
Pablo Neruda: I Explain a Few Things
The Collected Stories of Calvert Casey
Isaac Bashevis Singer: Collected Stories (3 volumes)
Cesar Chavez: An Organizer's Tale
Rubén Darío: Selected Writings
Pablo Neruda: All the Odes
Latin Music (2 volumes)
Words in Transit

GENERAL

The Essential Ilan Stavans

The Oven

AN ANTI-LECTURE

Ilan Stavans

Photographs by Bill Hughes

University of Massachusetts Press
AMHERST AND BOSTON

Printed in the United States of America
ISBN *978-1-62534-358-1 (paper)*
Designed by Kristina Kachele Design, llc
Set in Chaparrel Pro with Isodora Sans display
Printed and bound by Sheridan Books, Inc.
Cover design by Kristina Kachele Design, llc
Cover photo by Bill Hughes.

Library of Congress Cataloging-in-Publication Data
A catalog record for this book is available from the Library of Congress.

British Library Cataloguing-in-Publication Data
A catalog record for this book is available from the British Library.

Para mi padre

Contents

Things fall apart; the centre cannot hold;
Mere anarchy is loosed upon the world.
—William Butler Yeats, “The Second Coming” (1919)

The Oven

The Oven

(Lights on. The stage is empty except for a coat-rack and a small table, behind which is a chair. On the table there is a pitcher and an empty water glass. Enter a fifty-year-old man. He takes his jacket off and hangs it up. In a meditative mood, he relocates the chair to the center and sits in it.)

"An unexamined life is not worth living."

I read, years ago, a book—a memoir—by George Steiner. He is an American essayist, translator, and philosopher born in Paris, the author of *After Babel.* He once said, "We know that a man can read Goethe or Rilke in the evening, that he can play Bach and Schubert, and go to his day's work at Auschwitz in the morning." Steiner's work makes me uncomfortable. He is aloof, presumptuous, condescending. Whenever I finish a piece by him, I have the impression he thinks he's superior to his readers. Maybe he is, but should he brag about it? He is one of those writers I often read *against,* to find out not so much what he says but what I think about it. That's one cardinal sin in literature I can't fathom: an author with a superiority complex. Anyway, Steiner's memoir is called *Errata.* He was almost seventy when he published it. The subtitle is *An Examined Life.* It's a play on a line by Socrates, which I very much like. In fact, I adhere to it wholeheartedly. "An unexamined life is not worth living."

(*Pours water and drinks it.*)

Socrates is one of three martyrs; the other two are Jesus and Buddha. Each of the three represents a distinct type of martyrdom. Jesus's plight is about love of neighbor. Buddha's is about inner peace. And Socrates—he is about intellectual dissent. Do you know why Socrates drank the hemlock? The answer: he was known for perverting the Athenian youth. But what kind of perversion was he guilty of? This is rather complicated, but it boils down to his attitude: he didn't comply with the status quo. Democracy is messy because the citizens have personal views. They don't want to be sheep. They want an option. And options are born from exploration. Socrates believed that an examined life might, on occasion, take you into a realm you're unfamiliar with. If your search is authentic, exploring that realm is crucial.

Think about it. What is an unexamined life? What is the use of examining one's life, time and again? To see its motifs, its drive from a clearer perspective, I guess. Can a life—a whole life—be truly examined? We only understand who we are in retrospect, as we look at where we've been, what we've done. The present is where things always happen. Not in the past. Not in the future. Someone said to me: "the past is tense, the future is perfect." In the present, though, everything is in a state of fluidity. Our life is an accumulation of presents. Making sense of those coordinates is a challenge. And that challenge is what Socrates is after—having the guts to examine one's life as it unravels before us. Because, in truth, we only look back, creating connections between certain episodes and not others. Others we disregard, we forget. The ones we connect, we shape a narrative with. And that narrative justifies us. To make sense of the present, though, that's a challenge.

Steiner reduces everything to language. That's fine. I do, too. Yet language, as he argues, "only deals meaningfully with a special, restricted segment of reality. The rest, and it is presumably the much larger part, is silence." At one point in *Errata,* he says that he regrets never having tried LSD. I read the book years ago. If I remember right, a friend had offered it to him. It was probably the sixties. Stuffy as Steiner always was—an elitist, really!—he rejected the invitation. It made him anxious, afraid. He felt he wouldn't be in control, he felt he could lose it. So he passed. But in a strange way, he always regretted the decision. He felt his mind, as he matured, had known many things. Intellectually, the mind had been most fertile. He had delivered lectures, published essays, reflected on the classics. His mind had been prone to insight. But Steiner had never known one thing, how the world looks through LSD.

(*Sits down.*)

In telling this anecdote, Steiner, I think, was talking about cowardice. And about self-control. Making sense of who we are is about control: control of the narrative we shape in order to convince ourselves that we are still who we say we are. Being ourselves is having control of our own limits. Losing control is breaking those limits.

I don't remember much else about *Errata,* but Steiner's reference to LSD lives in my mind. It has its own room there. I occasionally enter that room. For years I had a similar regret. In part, mine is connected to my Jewish upbringing in Mexico. My mother, the rationalist in the family, frequently talked to me about the word—the concept—of *kashrut,* purity. She didn't only relate it to dietary law. In her view, it related to purity in general. It's your body that is kosher, Ilan. What you eat is a start. Yet it needs to go further. Kashrut is about how you protect the integrity of your body. No tattoos, no stimulants. The body does on its own what the body does.

(*Stands up again. Drinks more water.*)

I grew up with Jewish rituals. All of our neighbors were Catholic. On one occasion, one of them invited me to church. I saw how different it was to the place my family prayed in, a synagogue built in the shadow of the Holocaust. I also remember neighbors who weren't Catholic. Or better, who were

Catholic only superficially, that is, they were some kind of crypto-Catholics. They were *mestizos* although at heart they were indigenous. They practiced ancestral indigenous rituals. I was fascinated by their so-called pagan rites. Something about them made me feel like an anthropologist. As a Mexican, I felt it my duty to know more about these practices. But whatever I ended up knowing, it was always from an outsider's perspective. Call it a tourist's viewpoint. More to the point, why do people need rituals?

(*Pause.*)

By trade, I am a teacher. I didn't mean to become one. When I was young, I wanted to be an architect, a filmmaker, an explorer. Anything but a teacher. Not that the teachers I had were bad. I remember a few of them fondly. I wouldn't be the person that I am now without their lessons. But what they did day-to-day wasn't enticing to me. Life and adventure were outdoors, not in the classroom.

I became a teacher by happenstance. One day I got a job in a school. "Here's the textbook," I was told. "You start tomorrow at eight in the morning!" I hardly had time to think of what I was about to teach and if that was who I wanted to be.

From then on, things happened rather quickly. One class after another. Literature. This graduation and the next and another one. Suddenly, I realized I liked what I was doing. Teaching was magical. I could spend my hours exploring a certain theme, looking at it from every side. I could initiate a new generation in a literary classic, showing them why it matters. And I could learn as I taught.

It was a joyful journey. Until it wasn't. I would enter the classroom, look at the students' faces, and tell myself, "Okay, what kind of performance will you enact today in front of this crowd?" I was used to delving into a variety of topics, engaging people in insightful conversations. But then came time for exams. Or for final papers. And I felt bored. There's something dutiful about these activities. Students hate them and teachers know it. The exams and the papers would pile up on my desk. I would give myself a deadline to read them. One week. Ten days. No matter the self-imposed deadline, I would circle around but wouldn't touch them. I would invent all sorts of alternative duties: clean the basement, write a letter to a long-lost friend. When I finally wrapped my mind about the effort, I would enter a zone. It wouldn't be me who was reading the students' work, it was a robot. Is this how they've processed the material? Sharp. Thought-provoking. But ouch, the writing! It was boring as hell.

Or else, I would ask myself: How many times can you teach Cervantes's *Don Quixote?* From how many different perspectives? How about giving quantum physics a try? In the field of science, you're an ignoramus. But at least you'll approach it with fresh eyes. Repetition is the mother of doom.

I knew the classroom was my anchor. But was I stuck? After a couple of decades, it all became inevitably mechanical. People shouldn't do the same thing their entire life. It will suck the joy out of them. Even teaching. They should take a break. Not a month. Not a year. A sustained break. They should travel. Live in another country. That was the feeling I had; I dreamed of getting lost in the jungle. Anything but being in the classroom.

(*Pause again.*)

It wasn't only my teaching where I was at a crossroads. In my overall life, too. I was happily married. I had two bright, passionate boys. But you know how routine is: you wake up in the morning, take a shower, drive one kid to school, write a report of some sort, respond to email requests, answer the phone, lead a staff meeting, pick up the other kid from practice. Blah-blah-blah. Life is made of details. But those details get lost in the repetition. You end up playing your own role, becoming an actor in your own narrative.

Still, when asked I responded, "I'm happy." And I was, really. Aren't there different kinds of happiness? I'm talking about one that touches the surface. I thought I was leading a rational life, engaged, serene, wholesome. Of course, at some point evidence of the disquiet came pounding down on me. There was something fidgety in the air, something ominous. As if a rupture was about to take place. Or maybe a rapture.

The story I am about to tell, or at least part of it, takes place in Colombia's Amazon jungle. It is the story of a defeat. It ends in fracture. Yet it is also a story pregnant with meaning. I was in the middle of a tour throughout South America paid for by the U.S. State Department. Sorry to say but it was your tax money and mine. Up and down and up and down again. It was a frantic schedule: from Ecuador to Bolivia, from Guatemala to Peru, from Colombia to I don't remember where else. I would arrive in a city, be picked up by a chauffeur, deliver a lecture at a university, meet with some reporters, visit a community center, go to sleep, have breakfast, be taken to a high school, have lunch with the cultural attaché. Most of the time I was exhausted. I hardly had any chance to meet people. You know what I mean—to connect, to feel that people were living bodies with fears, with pride, with dreams.

On a given day, I found myself in Bogotá delivering a lecture. I forget what this one in particular was about. After the lecture, people surrounded me. They wanted to ask a question, to take a *selfie,* to give me a present. I noticed a tall, slim man a few steps away from me. He had long brown hair, a goatee, was wearing a leather vest and a baseball cap. He was waiting for his turn.

"*Hola, Profe,*" he said. He called me *profe,* just like my students do. But he was older, in his early forties. "My name is Benjamín." And he added a few other things, that he was a photographer and a performance artist, and that his studio wasn't far away. And that maybe I would want to have a cup of coffee with him.

At first I try to be grateful when invitations such as this come up. But I quickly apologize with whatever excuse crosses my mind. However, for some reason I couldn't this time around. To this day I don't know why. Why, with such fatigue, would I say yes to an absolute stranger? Well, there was something in Benjamín, something I can't explain. In his midthirties, he was tall and slim. He wore jeans and a T-shirt. He was relaxed in a Zen-like way. To me, he looked like a young, modern version of Don Quixote. I empathized with him immediately. He seemed like a gentleman. You know, we have deprived the word *gentleman* of its meaning. He was one, I thought. Why not relax in front of a stranger with a cup of good coffee?

I finished my business at the lecture. He told me he would wait for me in a café and gave me the address. Fifteen minutes later, I found him there. He smiled and so did I. We began a conversation. Soon we were talking about all sorts of things. Benjamín told me he was a shaman. He had been raised among the Putumayo. He had moved to Bogotá to do photography. He showed me a few pictures on his iPhone. I loved them. Then he invited me to visit his studio. I agreed.

I found myself in it an hour later. Benjamín's studio was in an old factory, more precisely, in a storage room mostly made of wood. Reclined on the wall were dozens of enlarged photographs, a few in color, most in black and white. He talked to me about intervening in them in all sorts of ways, spraying them with aerosol paints, sticking expired credit cards to them, or scratching them with a fork. He disliked the word *photoshop*. "My objective," he said, "is to turn an image into a dream."

Among Benjamín's many images I saw was one I was particularly struck by. It was in color and depicted the interior of a hut. The floor was just soil. The walls were made of dry palm leaves, as was the roof. In the middle of the hut was a stool on which an old woman sat patiently. She was dressed in black. Her hair was long, so long it reached her ankles. She looked attentively into a small fire near her. The yellows and reds and oranges and blues of the fire were vivid. And here's what made the picture dreamlike: directly on top of the old woman was a canoe. The canoe was suspended in the air. It was painted in different colors. Above it was a flock of butterflies.

It made no sense. The canoe had no reason to be floating. But it did. Was this a hallucination? As if wanting an explanation, I looked at Benjamín. He smiled but didn't say a thing.

A few minutes later, we talked about religion. He asked me if I was a believer. I told him I was Jewish. For some reason, my answer made me think of the synagogue I attended when I was young. It was a regular synagogue. During the service, the rabbi would ask the congregation to stand up. So we all stood up. After reading a passage in the liturgy, he would ask everyone to sit down. So we sat down. I remember that repetitive motion: standing up, sitting down, standing up, sitting down . . . Benjamín asked me if I believed in God. "I do," I said, "although I can't quite describe my God." He said his tribe would love to host me one day in a shamanic ceremony in the Amazon.

I thanked him. "Maybe one day," I responded, knowing full well I would never engage in such an activity. I hadn't done it in Mexico as I was growing up. Why would I suddenly do it in Colombia? And with a stranger? Plus, I had a hectic schedule. I needed to wake up early next morning to go to the airport. "Well, if you change your mind, or if you come back to Bogotá and have three or four days for yourself, just call me a bit in advance." He said this as he wrote his phone number on the back of a restaurant bill. "You just need to be ready internally . . ."

I knew that what Benjamín meant by "being ready" was about letting myself go, about not being in control, about allowing my senses, not my intellect, to lead the way. You see, I find myself thinking all the time. I think that I think. I see others think and I wonder what they are thinking. I also ask myself, are we all one of God's thoughts? Will we disappear the moment He stops thinking of us?

The way Benjamín phrased the invitation, it felt as a *fait accompli*. I don't know . . . I really wasn't free to say no. But, honestly, I didn't want to be free.

Three weeks later, I landed in Bogotá again. This was still part of my lecture itinerary. For some unexplained reason, as soon as I made it to the airport, I left a message on Benjamín's voice mail. It was Thursday, I think. I said I had several days before returning home. I really didn't have any of those days. My next flight was tomorrow. But when Benjamín called back saying he would pick me up at my hotel at nine that night, I made arrangements to switch my return home. What I didn't do was call Alison, my wife, or Bobbie, my secretary, to cancel my classes for the following day. Why didn't I? I don't know. I wouldn't have known what excuse to give. Or maybe because I didn't think Benjamín would pick me up.

I ate and took a shower. Shortly before nine the phone rang. I looked at it. Don't answer, I told myself. I realized I was trembling. You don't have to go, I said again. Don't do it.

In the end, I did pick up the phone. "*Hola.*" "*Profe,* how are you? It's Benjamín. *Me da gusto oir su voz.*" After the conversation, I was still unsure. Should I go or should I stay? I put my jacket on and took it off. I untied and retied my shoes. Had I brushed my teeth? I did it again, just in case. Five, ten, fifteen minutes went by, until I opened the door to the room, took the elevator, and made my way down.

Benjamín and another man were waiting for me. "*Profe, gusto en verlo.* This is my brother Tomás. Did you eat? The SUV is waiting for us . . ." As we walked outside, I noticed it was a bit cold. I said I needed to get a jacket. "*No se preocupe, Profe,*" said Benjamín. "We have plenty of blankets."

(*Looks at the empty glass.*)

Tomás opens the door of the SUV. Inside are several people. The darkness makes it difficult for me to discern more than silhouettes. Several of them greet me. I respond in kind. Tomás takes the driver's seat and Benjamín the copilot's. He hands me a lunch box. "*Es pa' usted.*" It is meant for you, he says.

The SUV starts to move. People talk to one another. Someone asks me if I am Colombian. I open the lunch box. There is a sandwich, an apple, and a bottle of water.

(*Walks around.*)

The SUV drives for hours. I fall asleep after a while. I assume others do, too.

We leave the city behind. Then another city, and another. Every so often I look out: darkness. Finally, at dawn we arrive at a hacienda. It is in a clearing in the middle of a forest. The SUV stops. When I open my eyes fully, Benjamín is already outside. The door of the SUV opens up automatically and I come out. Before me I see a house made of big glass windows. It looks like a rural community center. I and others walk toward it. There is no furniture inside. I see a few buckets, toilet-paper rolls, supermarket bags with groceries, a broom, cleaning equipment, a few jackets, lots of blankets, and a box of candles.

Other people have been waiting for us. Benjamín's brother now has a guitar in hand. He talks to me about his Amazonian tribe. He says his mother will participate in the ceremony.

Soon everyone walks to the other side of the house, which looks onto a large expanse of land. Far from us are the edges of the clearing, made of a curtain of trees. It must all be owned by the *hacendado,* I tell myself. In the middle of the clearing I see a traditional outdoor oven. It is about my height, made of stone and cement. Its mouth is dark. Near it I see lots of chopped wood.

We all walked in the direction of the oven. Someone has put wood inside to start a fire. People are now wrapped in blankets. The oven feels warm, inviting. No wonder it is the site around which everyone congregated. What time is it? I look at my watch. It is seven in the morning.

(*Takes off his watch and puts it away.*)

I take my watch off and put it inside my pocket.

(*Pause.*)

I look around. On the other side of the oven is an old woman dressed in black. She is sitting on a stool. His mother . . . It takes me a few seconds to realize it is the same person from the photograph Benjamín showed me in his studio in Bogotá. Tomás, just a few feet away from me, begins to play random notes on the guitar. "*Venga, Profe,*" he states. "I want to introduce you." I walk toward the *curandera,* who quickly makes a welcoming gesture.

"*Profe, nos alegra tenerlo entre nosotros.*" It is a pleasure having you with us. She and I talk for a few minutes while Tomás continues to play the guitar. "She's really proud you're here, *Profe,*" he announces a few minutes later. "She is the tribe's elder."

Near her is an altar. It is made of different layers. In it I see a crucifix, candles, black-and-white portraits, an assortment of fruits and nuts, and several cans of Coca-Cola. There are also a bunch of cups and a pitcher. I see someone bringing out the buckets and toilet paper from inside the building.

I notice that everyone—some twelve to fifteen people—have created a semicircle around the oven. They are sitting on the ground, patiently waiting. I do the same. I find a place near a young woman with curly hair. I wait, too.

The distance between us and the house is about a mile.

(*Sits down. Takes his shoes off.*)

I am wearing jeans, a sweater, and sneakers. My five o'clock shadow is beginning to show. When will the ceremony start? Someone offers me a blanket. I say I'm not cold. Benjamín's brother plays his guitar more emphatically. Everyone is silent. The soil under me feels wet. It probably rained the night before.

What kind of ceremony exactly am I attending? It becomes clear to me that the musical repertoire is stubbornly inadequate. It isn't songs Tomás is playing but random, inharmonious rhythms. The constant, seemingly endless repetition of them is obnoxious.

As I listen, I catch myself thinking. And thinking. It's a complex web of thoughts. Ideas within ideas. A relentless stream. The guitar notes expand in my mind. They acquire some kind of physical presence. I feel I'm a victim of trying to understand too much, of forcing my mind to make sense of everything.

At this point the *curandera* makes a gesture, asking me to come near her. She pours a potion from the pitcher into a cup.

(*Moves around. Pours water into glass.*)

She says it was *ayahuasca.* I have never heard the word before. Never. In my mind, the syllables come apart: *a-ya-huas-ca, a-ya-huas-ca.* The *curandera* hands me the cup. Wait—should I research its contents? I'm the type of person who is meticulous about anything he puts inside his stomach. Should I reject the drink? I really didn't know what I'm about to ingest. I think: "I'm here under the auspices of the U.S. State Department. Am I doing something wrong? Is taxpayer's money being misused?"

It crosses my mind that ayahuasca is a hallucinogenic brew. Only later do I find out that people also call it *yagé* and it is used for divinatory purposes, like healing and prophesies. It is made of leaves of shrubs and a plant known as *Justicia pectoralis.* It contains DMT, which is a psychedelic compound of the tryptamine family.

(*Pours more water.*)

I drink it!

(*Drinks.*)

Yak!

It is a thick, gluey liquid, like unprocessed petroleum. The taste is disgusting . . .

(*Spits.*)

"*Profe, Profe,* don't spit it. And don't taste it either. You won't like it. You shouldn't taste it. Just ingest it!" She says the effect will start in a few minutes.

I gulp the whole cup.

(*Sits down on the chair, is uncomfortable, and then sits on the floor.*)

I go back to the place I have been sitting. And I wait again. Socrates's line flashes in my mind: "An unexamined life is not worth living." This isn't a ceremony. There is nothing structured about it. Then I think of how I like to portray myself as an outsider. Nowadays it is something of a stretch, but when I was young such attitude made sense to me. If you saw me alone at a party, you would think that I'm not a social type, that I'm aloof, coy, reticent. Whenever I arrived, I would look around, reach for a beer, and find a corner from which I would be able to observe. That is what I did at parties: observe. Was I having a good time? Yes, although my idea of a good time was perhaps different from that of others.

With the Putumayo now, I again tell myself: "While you're not young any more, you're still an observer. Actually, call yourself an anthropologist. Didn't you come to the Amazon this time by accident? It is too late to retrace your steps. Think of what is taking place before your eyes—a *happening.* Once you reach home, you'll transform that happening into a story. That's what you always do. And that's where the value of this whole experience is: as inspiration. The potion you just drank . . . Was it hemlock? Don't worry, it won't have any effect on you, just like the beers at those parties never got you drunk. You just pretended to be, didn't you? A performer. In order not to make others uncomfortable, this time you should pretend again. Come on! Be an actor. You love to play a role, don't you?"

Should I have phoned Alison to tell her I would be away? I feel guilty. She won't know where I am and will be worried. And should I have called the secretary? This is irresponsible. I'm a public figure. What if I get caught doing all this?

Ay! Tomás keeps repeating the same notes again and again. Then it crosses my mind; he isn't really a musician. His guitar playing is meant as an anchor. The repetition of sounds is heard by everyone. It creates a sense of community.

One by one, the other participants take their turn approaching the *curandera*. They are Putumayo, they know what they're doing. She hands them their potion and they drink it without complaint. Soon I can see the immediate effect on them. Some begin to look as if they are no longer themselves; others stare at a blank space and laugh; still others stand up as if pushed by an urge and wander into the woods. Benjamín follows the few who abandon the flock. He gives them blankets.

But nothing is happening to me.

Suddenly, I become hungry. I look around for a piece of meat. None to be found. Near the oven I see a loaf of bread.

(*Runs. Pretends to hold an item. Contorts.*)

To my right, the woman with curly hair abruptly rushes to where a bucket is and vomits. It is as if a demon has taken over her.

Then, a big, bulky guy, whose sense of humor I enjoyed before—he introduced himself as Jesus in the SUV—unexpectedly collapses onto the ground, face down.

He looks dead. Benjamín comes to him, makes sure he is breathing, puts a blanket on top, and leaves him alone. Those of us who are near approached Jesus, hold hands, and start singing. The song, I don't know why. The song reminds me of a joyful prayer I used to hear in synagogue. Now it feels like a funeral. Is Jesus dead?

I become scared and return to my place. Swiftly, without explanation, I think of the glasses I'm wearing. They might break at any point. I need to put them in a safe place. Where? I should give them to Benjamín's mother. She will know what to do with them.

(*Stands up.*)

I walk toward her. "*Venga, Profe.* Are you okay? Do you want more ayahuasca?" I take my glasses off and hand them to her. She smiles as she places them on the altar. As I walk back to my place again, I'm invaded by a peaceful inner sensation.

(*Sits.*)

Oh, my! My glasses. From where I sit I try to look at them. How embarrassing! I can't see a thing. It becomes obvious that I left my eyes with the glasses. You need to get up, I tell myself. You need to get your eyes.

I feel hot. Very hot. As if I'm sweating.

(*Takes shirt off.*)

But I'm not sweating.

(*Pause.*)

Ouch. I can't stand on my feet. As I approach the *curandera,* I am on all fours. And I look for a bucket because . . .

(*Vomits.*)

Everyone is looking at me. But I am not myself, not anymore. My skin begins to change. I feel a thin layer of fur on top of it. My hands, they look like paws. I see my nails become sharper. And my mouth, it is the mouth of a jaguar. I have a feline appearance.

(Moves like jaguar.)

Odd, I tell myself. I'm a beast. I can't be a beast.

Can I be a jaguar? In fact, I have been a jaguar forever.

(Howls.)

I look at the *curandera,* who gives me yet another reassuring smile.

(Jumps onto the table. Roars. Flies across the stage. Runs like a feline. Pretends to eat his own shoe.)

I race across the clearing. For hours, maybe days.

(Sits down. Contorts.)

Sounds are really loud.

I am cold. I need protection. Near the oven, I feel heat. And I eat a deer. Leisurely.

(Pretends to devour animal.)

Magically, while absorbing heat, my molecules begin to . . . disperse. My body loses its contours.

(Makes ethereal gestures.)

Each cell becomes free, part of a swirl. I am a small tornado pullulating on the air, on top of the trees, across the hacienda, free to roam without obstacle.

I then see the oven again. I am overwhelmed by a desire to rotate around it, to caress its surface.

(*Pretends to embrace the structure.*)

I look at the oven's mouth. I smell the inside. Then, KABOOM, I make my way into it. I am in the oven's inner chamber. The fire is burning before me. The fire is burning me. My molecules touch the heated walls of brick. I am the oven. The fire is inside me.

(*Struggles to regain control.*)

A line in Hebrew, from the Talmud, comes to mind: "*Nitzjuni banai.*" Where have I read it? What does it mean? I think and think.

I remember my ancestors who died in gas chambers and their bodies were incinerated by the Nazis in ovens. I see their faces popping up from the fire. They come to me, they whisper in my ear. Yes, we are in conversation. But in what language are they speaking? I don't understand a word. What are they saying? They need me. They want me. They are happy to have me.

(Breathes heavily.)

After a few minutes, maybe a millennium, I see two men, inside the oven chamber, one on each side of the fire. They are dressed in black pants and white shirts, have *payes* and *tsitsis,* and wear *yarmulkes.* I look at them attentively. They are identical. They must be twins.

The rabbis are in the middle of an argument. Each of them, on their forehead, has an assortment of numbers written on it. They are in red. The numbers appear to descend at rapid speed: 437, 436, 435, 434 . . .

They are talking about an oven.

(*Jumps frantically from one side to another.*)

The rabbi to my right, Rabbi Eliezer, says the oven is forever kosher because it has been consecrated with purified tools. He stresses the word *forever.* The rabbi to my left, Rabbi Yehoshua, says no: if the oven at any point is dismantled, it will no longer be kosher. Rabbi Eliezer says it *is* kosher. Rabbi Yehoshua says it *isn't* kosher. Back and forth, back and forth.

Where do I stand? Do I agree with one?

Then Rabbi Eliezer says: "The universe is full. No matter what humans do to it, it will always be full. It depends on us to find its fullness." Rabbi Yehoshua replies: "No, the universe is broken. It has always been broken. We can't fix it even if we want to. God had a mission and we spoil it." Back and forth between these two views. Back and forth.

Rabbi Eliezer says: "Not only am I right. God is on my side."

"Ridiculous," says Rabbi Yehoshua. "How can you claim that God is on your side? Who knows on what side God stands?"

Rabbi Eliezer says: "As proof of His endorsement, God will make this fire disappear."

"I don't care if God makes the fire disappear," says Rabbi Yehoshua. "This is a human argument, not a divine one."

(*Screams. Jumps. Screams again.*)

At this point I think of *Julius Cesar,* Shakespeare's play, where Cassius says to Brutus: "The fault, dear Brutus, is not in our stars. But in ourselves."

"Nah," posits Rabbi Eliezer. "All arguments are divine." Rabbi Yehoshua: "All arguments are human."

(*At height of emotion.*)

Back and forth, back and forth.

Inside the oven's chamber, a deep, larger-than-life, overwhelming laugher is heard: "HA, HA, HA . . . *Nitzjuni banai. Nitzjuni banai."* It is Hebrew. It means "My children have betrayed me." "My children have betrayed me."

(*Falls into ground in trance as strident noise is heard.*)

"¡Ramera! ¡Cabrona!" Someone is screaming from afar. *"¡Puta! ¡Traicionera!"*

"Profe, Profe . . ." Benjamín is tapping my back. "*Profe,* we need to go."

"What's happening, Benjamín?"

"We need to go, *Profe*. The police might be coming. The ex-husband of the hacienda owner is furious that she allowed us to spend these days here."

I look around. It is pitch black. People start to run for shelter. I ask myself if I should, too. For a moment I think that what's happening was a figment of my imagination. The screaming man is now throwing stones at us. One of them hits the oven, another breaks a glass window. My heart is beating fast. I see a blanket flying. And another. People are running fast.

"*Profe,* please get into the SUV. Everything will be alright," he says. Ah, the dirty business of life.

(*Relaxes on chair.*)

I woke up in my hotel. I don't remember how I got there. I had a terrible headache. My stomach hurt. I ran to the toilet, back and forth, back and forth. My entire body was in shock.

My heart was beating fast, very fast. Too fast. I was furious. I wanted to get out of my own skin.

(*Puts shirt on, shoes, jacket, and watch.*)

Benjamín called to make sure I was okay. He apologized. I told him there was nothing to apologize for.

The whole episode took three days. I was miserable. I flew back home in a state of despondency.

As I mentioned at the outset, this is the story of a defeat. But there are defeats more valuable than triumphs. The ceremony I had participated in had been interrupted abruptly. The feeling I had was of having been aborted, of having been pushed out of a cocoon. Still, there was something edifying, something impossible to articulate, that was immensely liberating.

It took me a while to tell Alison the story. She was angry with me for not having phoned her. When I explained the details, she was even more upset. Only after a few days did she calm down. "Why did you need to participate in such a ritual?" she asked.

Of course, the response I got from my two adolescent boys was totally different: "When can we try it, Pa?"

In the days and weeks to come, my understanding of everything would change. I would become more attuned to sounds, gestures, emotions. I would listen to people more carefully. I would be more patient. And I would cherish silence.

Silence in the classroom acquired heightened tones. Teachers in general are afraid of silence. It is uncomfortable. It means people aren't saying anything, which means they don't know something. But silence is sound. Silence is knowledge. In groups, silence denotes a way to think collectively. And the teacher's silence—it is a sign of respect.

I was eager to return to my students. Should I tell them what I had been through? Yes, without reservations. I wanted to be vulnerable before them. I wanted to show that I am also fragile like them, weak. That I don't have all the answers.

The following morning, I made it back to school. It was a misty morning. It had rained the night before. Everything looked shiny, as if someone had polished reality to make it seem new.

As I walked across campus, one of my students saw me from afar. "*Profe, Profe,* you're back. I'm happy! Are you okay?" She was thrilled to see me. I was too. In fact, I couldn't wait to get back into class.

I was taken by a vigorous force inside. It was a force that told me that I should be in front of my students. It told me that I wanted to teach again.

I wanted to see Alison, to hug her, to walk through town with her. I wanted to see the faces of my two boys. To see them giggle.

And I thought about George Steiner and about how making sense of who we are is about control. About self-control. The rest was visceral . . .

The student and I talked for a little while. I notice that on her forehead was a line of numbers. In red. They were declining in size: 1,002,993, 1,002,872, 1,002,795 . . . Every time she said a word, the amount would go down a digit. It finally dawned on me: we are all born with a number in our forehead. That number is the total amount of words we have been allocated. Every time we use one, we lose it too. Death is the arrival of zero.

It is true: An unexamined life is not worth living.

(Exits. Lights off.)

Photographs by Bill Hughes

The Oven: An Anti-Lecture, at Double Edge,
Ashfield, Massachusetts, November 11 and 12, 2015.

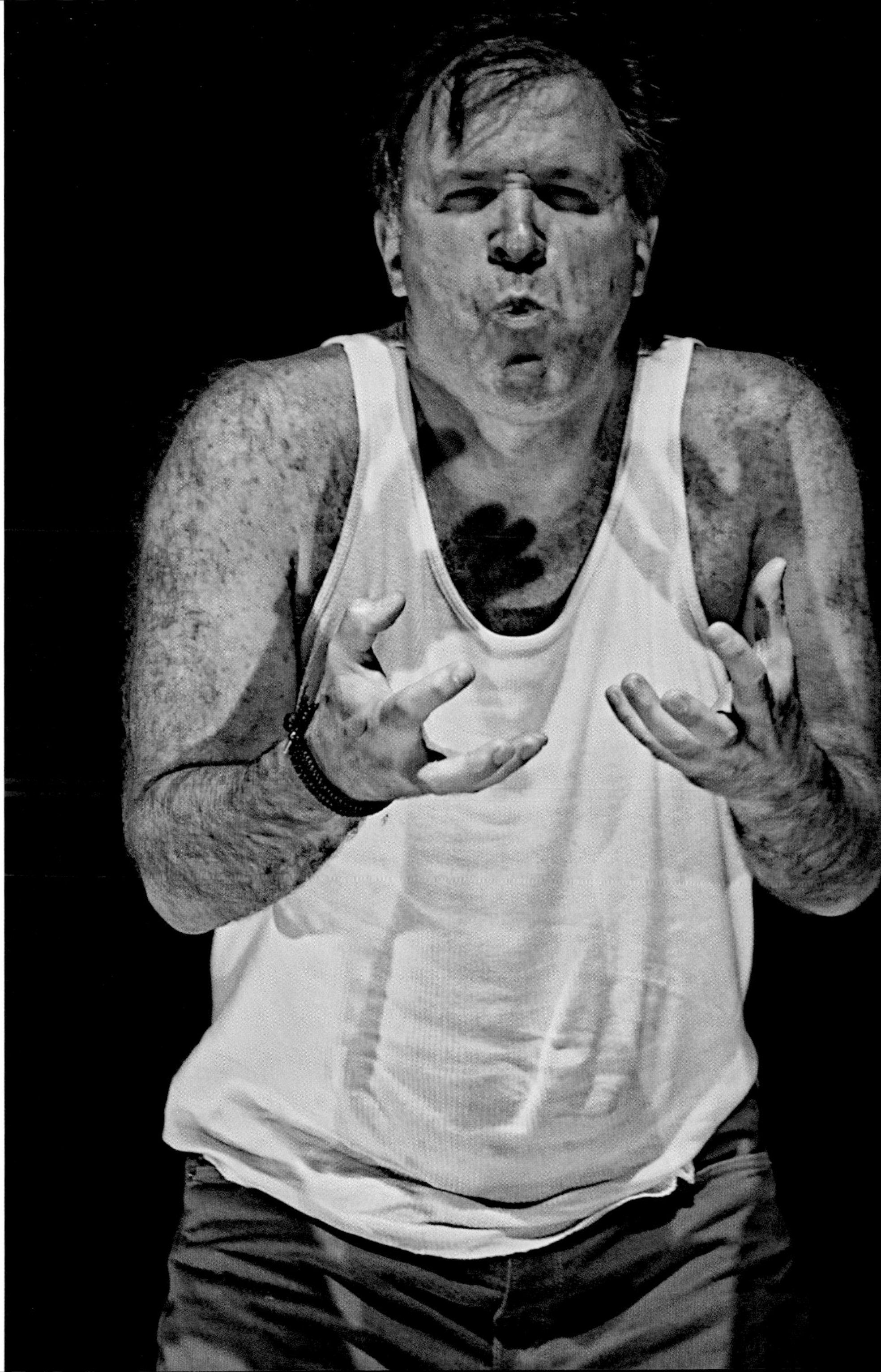

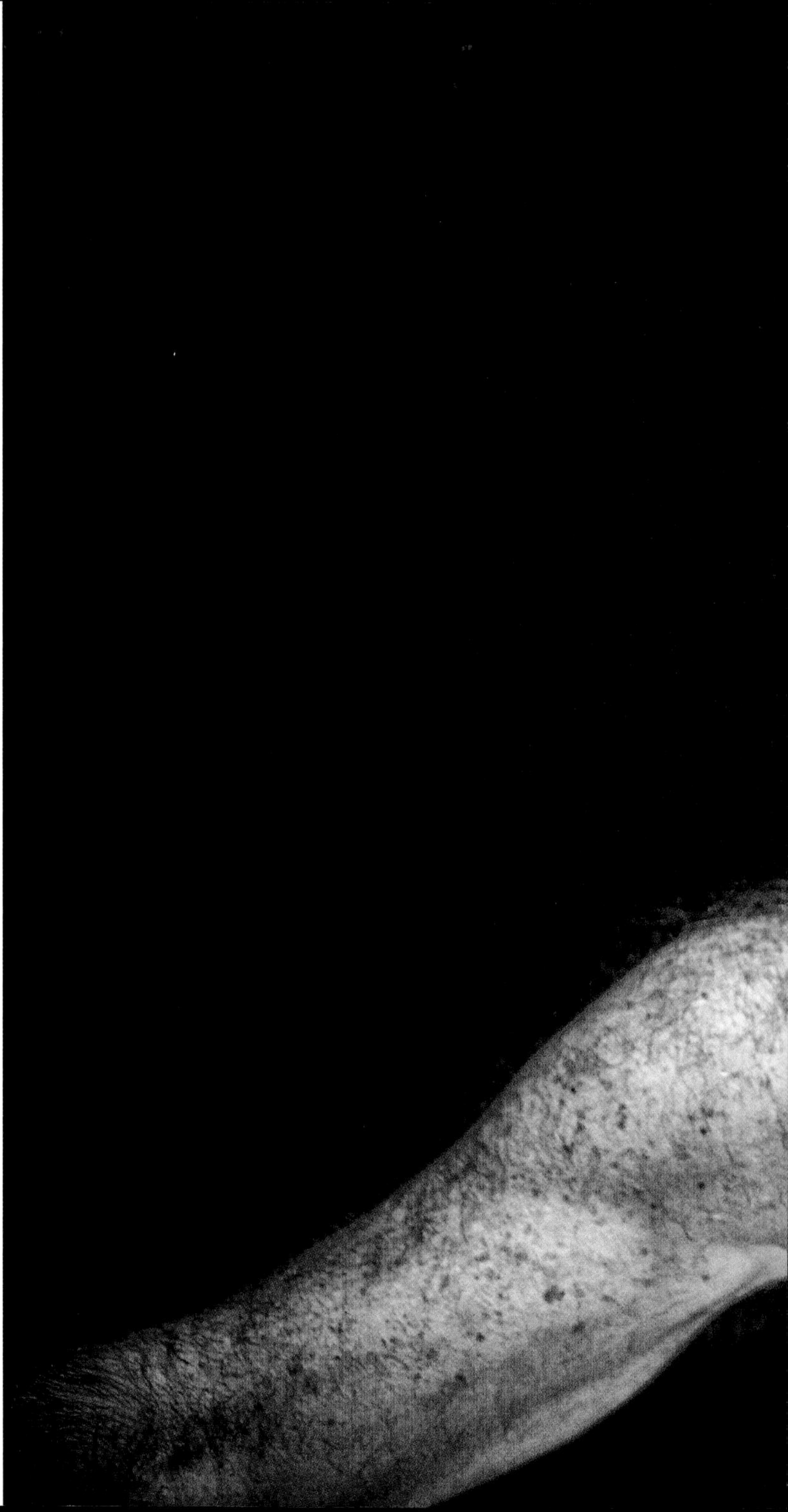

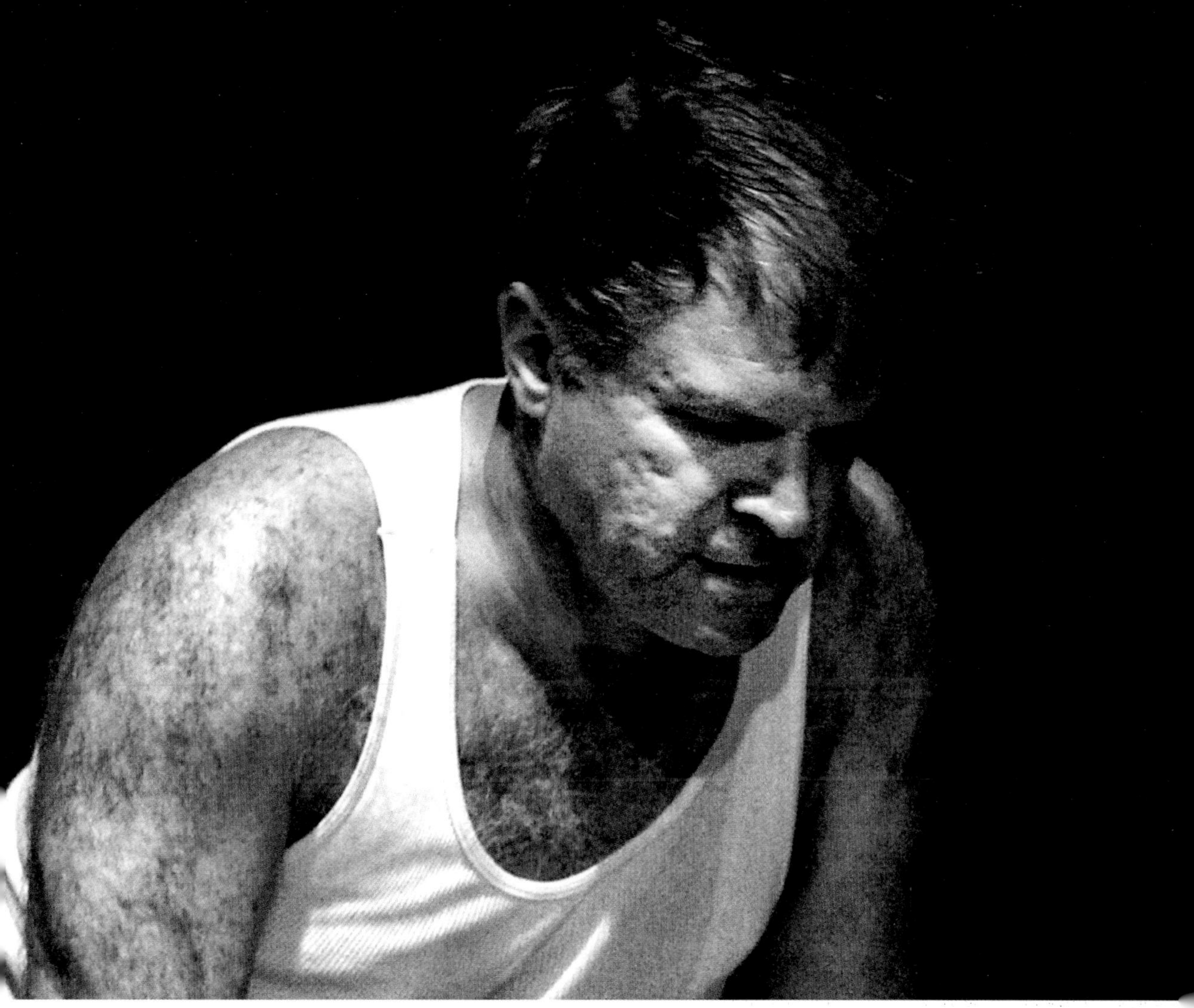

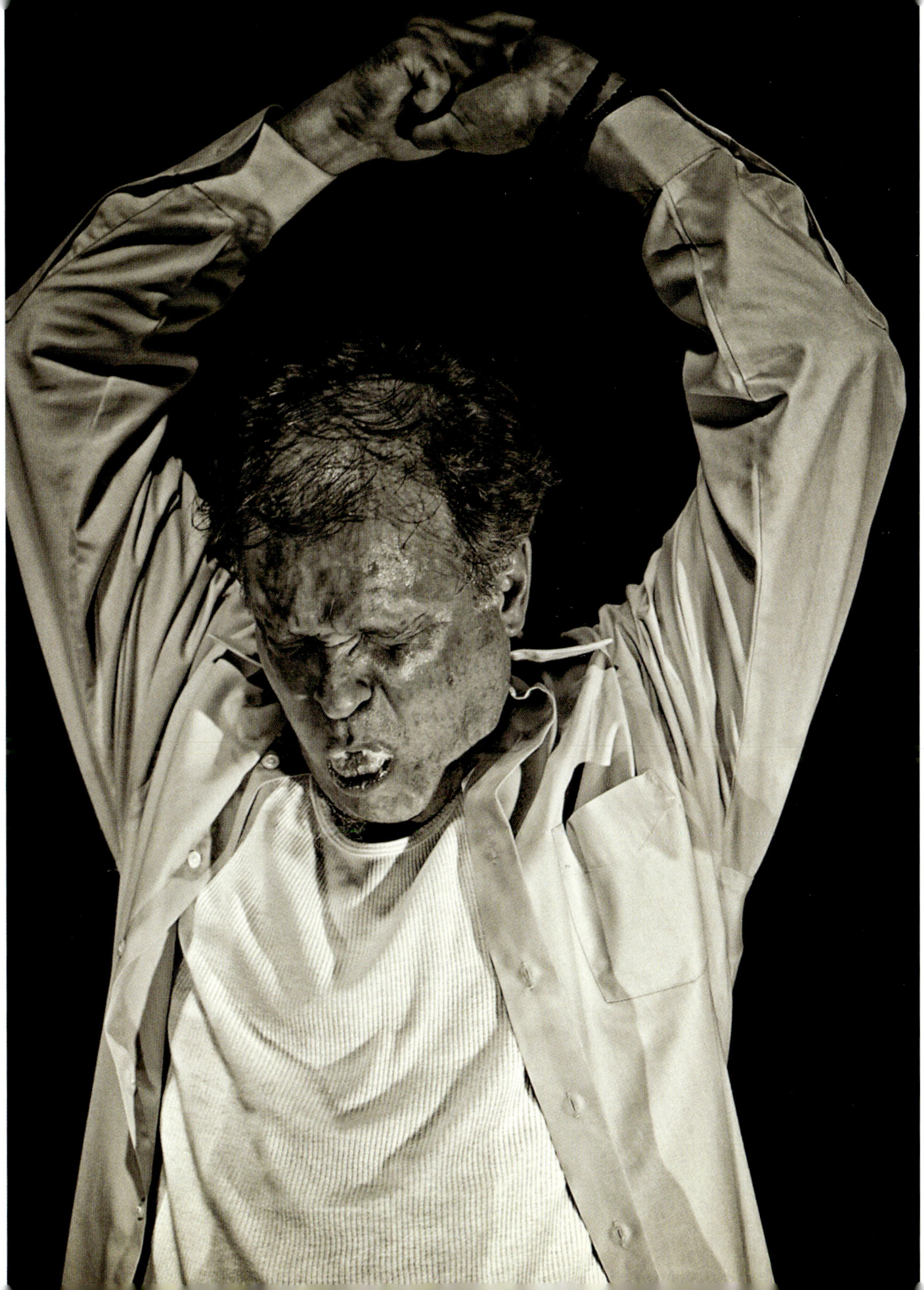

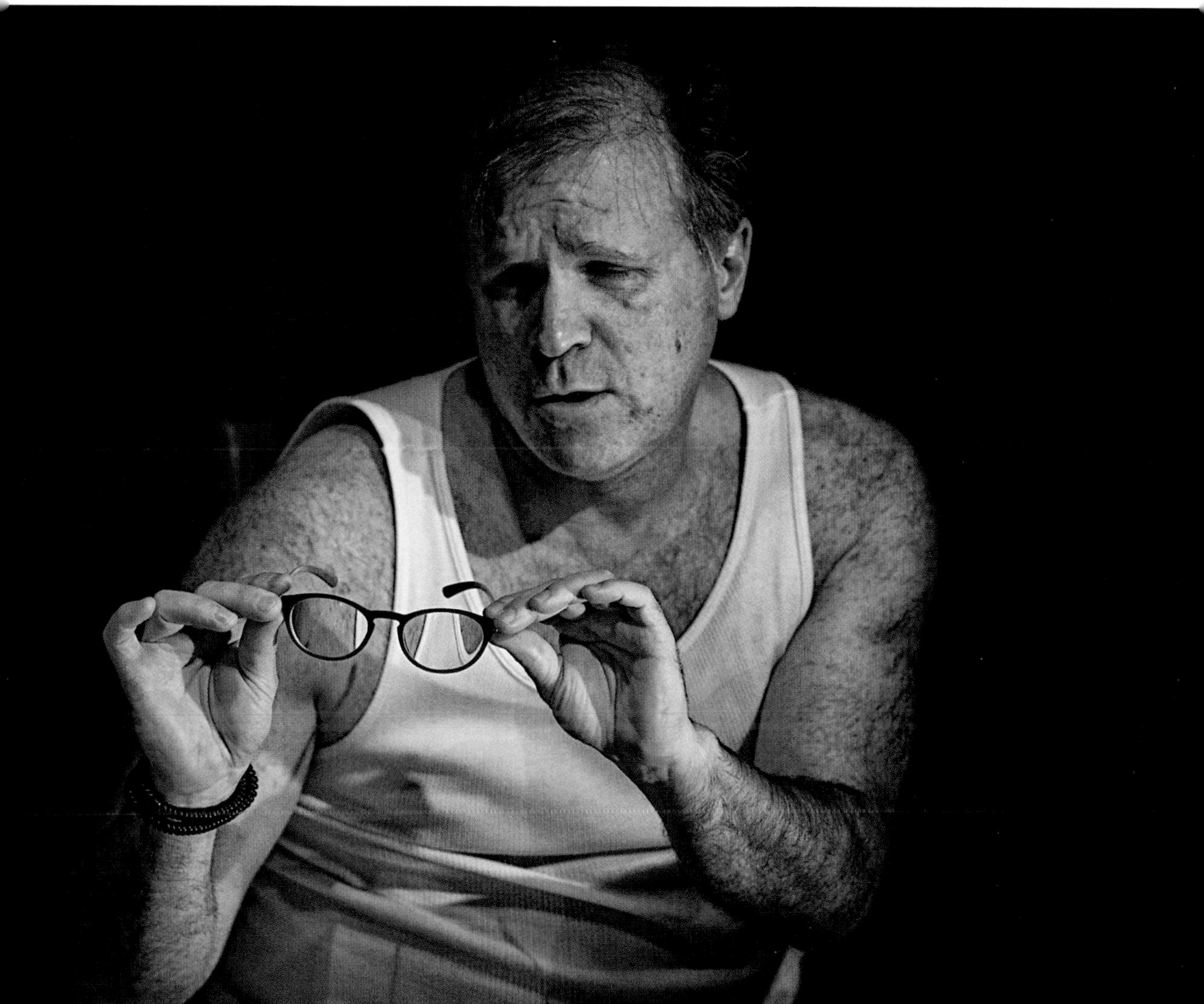

The Center Cannot Hold

After my return from the Amazon, I tried my luck chronicling what I had gone through, first through journalism, then as fiction. Nothing worked. Words were stumbling blocks. I remembered that before I departed Colombia, I had mentioned to Benjamín my desire to turn the experience into a narrative. He smiled. "Then you'll be betraying it," he said. "As an organizer of reality, language itself, most likely, will be useless to you." He added: "You're a teacher. You use words to convey different universes. Now use words to surrender."

It took me a while to understand what Benjamín meant. When I finally did, I realized that for it to tick, the narrative needed to be *live.* It needed to feel like a rite of passage. It needed to be performed in front of an audience. It needed to play with silences. And with the other side of words, which is sound. Words that sound but don't mean. Words that fill up the air. That transport us into unforeseen realms. Words that serve as conduits to the realm of magical thinking, where nothing is what it appears to be.

In *The Oven,* I described the mechanical state in which I found myself before my encounter with Benjamín in Bogotá and his invitation to join his mother, the *curandera,* in the religious ceremony. I said I was a teacher. A husband. A father. A happy man. Happy in outward ways. I probably should say now what I'm not—an actor. But I'm the son of one. My father shaped his career on TV and the movies. Yet theater was by far his favorite medium. Every year he was in at least a couple of shows. Some were traditional, others experimental.

As an adolescent, I would accompany him to his shows. Watching him behind the curtains, I would imagine myself in his shoes. This exercise made me fall in love with the mechanics of theater. Why have some cultures taken to theater while others haven't? How does an actor become someone else? To what extent is theater a religious ritual?

Expectedly, I too contemplated at one point a life on stage. But I gave up the idea. I was impatient with the collaborative aspect of plays. I loved words, not gestures. Yet as soon as I became a teacher, I realized it wasn't an either/or choice.

Teachers are actors. To keep students enthralled, one needs to do all sorts of pirouettes, intellectual as well as physical. Each session must be scripted yet remain jazzy, improvisational. Over the years, this realization became for me a compromise. Today I can't think of a more-rewarding way of spending my life than teaching. And because of that, I also think of myself as an actor.

By default, having failed at my attempts to write about what happened to me in the Amazon as prose, I started to reread Socrates. What did he stand for? Why did he antagonize Athenian society? Was his philosophy dangerous? In what way was dialogue his pedagogical tool? One of the books I opened was I. F. Stone's *The Trial of Socrates*. It felt fresh because Stone was a reporter, not a scholar. Socrates's downfall was delivered as a detective investigation.

What I liked the most, though, was Stone's suggestion that Socrates, while thinking aloud in front of his pupils, was a jester. His teaching, which ultimately led him to martyrdom, explored the limits of rationality.

If only I could do the same with magical thinking . . .

About forty-five minutes from where I live is Ashfield, Massachusetts, home to Double Edge, an experimental theater company. It is devoted to bringing down what Russian theater director Konstantin Stanislavski, in his book, *An Actor Prepares,* called "the fourth wall," the barrier between the actors and the audience. Its members live together on a farm in the old hill town, where their stage—a repurposed barn—sits. Any show they put on requires total commitment from cast and crew, including long hours of strenuous physical work to prepare.

Their spectacles take months to coalesce. When they do, the experience is exhilarating. Actors literally fly on stage from one end to another. They make themselves visible and invisible through harmonious rhythms that, structured around a loose plot and impressionistic music, transport the audience to another realm of perception. This is theater as ritual.

In 2007, Double Edge adapted one of my stories, "The Disappearance," about a Jewish actor in Belgium who, eager to denounce emerging neo-Nazi groups, plots his own kidnapping. The plot unfolds in semi-epistolary form. The company invited me to a small role in the play. I was thrilled to perform it.

Over the years, I became close to one of the Double Edge members, Matthew Glassman, an empathetic, versatile character actor and the company's co-director. I had seen Glassman play Sancho Panza in an adaptation of *Don Quixote,* in which he ate a large red raw onion on stage. He had also been Bruno Schultz, the Polish author, in *The Street of Crocodiles.* And he had played major roles in *The Odyssey, Arabian Nights,* and other theatrical adaptations of literary classics.

I proposed to Glassman the idea of turning my experience into a one-man play. I told him I wanted to work closely with him in my "crossing"—that is how I described it—and that I wanted to recreate the ceremony in a way that made it urgent, immediate. Glassman was on board right away.

It took months. He put me through intense physical training. Late at night at the barn, I ran like a lunatic to the rhythm of loud indigenous music. I jumped and screamed, laughed and cried until I fell flat on the floor with exhaustion. Slowly, a play started to birth, and my vulnerabilities as a Western-trained thinker were put to the test.

Unconsciously, in some mysterious way during the rehearsals, I became Glassman's student. Or maybe the word *student* is wrong. A pupil maybe.

Indeed, at various points he reminded me of Benjamín—gentle in his demeanor, Quixotic in his wisdom. I felt my capacity to learn undergo a cathartic change. Glassman would give me directions. I would follow them. But beyond his words, beyond his directions, lay a different kind of understanding I needed to unwrap by myself.

Strangely, performing the early versions of *The Oven* made me be a student in a unique classroom, an open, empty space demanding imagination—my imagination—to fill it.

Glassman envisioned a simple light and set design. The sole props on stage were a table, a chair, a hanger, a pitcher, and a glass of water. The rest were left to me as the performer. He convinced me that I must reconsider whatever decision I had made as a young man not to pursue acting. Or better yet, in alternative universes, the ones parallel to ours, some of those discarded options actually took place, and it was critical that I penetrate that universe to take command of my stage presence and own the space.

He also said that in order to bring audiences to the Amazon jungle, to make them experience the ritual themselves, I had to bridge the dichotomy Henry James once established between showing and telling, seamlessly confounding the line between describing what had happened and recreating it altogether.

We talked about Anton Chekhov's monologue "On the Harmful Effects of Tobacco." About Oliver Sacks's experimentations with LSD and other drugs. And about Spalding Gray, who I had seen perform his one-man shows, *Swimming to Cambodia* and *Monster in the Box,* at the Public Theater in Manhattan in the 1980s. Soon Glassman suggested we conceive of the play in which the fifty-year-old professor tests his own limits in ways that are at once embarrassing and enlightening. "Can you ridicule yourself as an academic while also celebrating the life of the mind, Ilan?" he asked.

Glassman suggested thinking of it as an "anti-lecture." It should be an exploration of the underbelly of the professoriate. The suggestion quickly resonated. I don't like it when people refer to me as an "academic." The term makes me feel detached from society. And "professor" is not much better. Professors are bluffs. We build a façade of impenetrability that hides our immense insecurities. We profess to love the intellect selflessly but seldom engage it fully because we are afraid to fail and we know any failure will be a public event. Freedom is wasted on us.

Within a couple of months of our collaboration, I wrote a first draft of the script. Putting words to paper this time around was unlike anything I had done before. Writers manipulate words to generate a certain effect. They craft their sentences in isolation, distant from what Thomas Hardy calls "the maddening crowd." Their hope is that one day those words will reach their destination, although they most likely never know who the addressee really is. The script of *The Oven* was altogether different. For one thing, the words were never fixed. Just the opposite, they felt ephemeral. What I would say in one rehearsal would change in the following one. Writing down my notes, I would attempt to find coherence in the overall enterprise. That coherence took time to show up.

But when it did, there was a feeling of purity in the whole narrative. Bertrand Russell said once that a hallucination is a fact, not an error. The theatrical piece that eventually emerged is autonomous, self-sufficient. It was and wasn't what had happened to me in Colombia. One hundred percent happened exactly as depicted on stage and one hundred percent didn't.

A regular performance of *The Oven* lasts approximately seventy-five minutes. The adjective *regular* is deceitful, though. While the core is the same, things are always changing. No two shows are alike. Even I surprise myself with the way the storyline is unstill, swirling. That's why I love performing it: it is as malleable, as perfect in its imperfections, as life itself. The shaman was right: As an organizer of reality, language is a traitor.

Of course, committing language to a book, as I have done now, is an even more foolish endeavor. Still, the written word is my currency. Theater takes place in the eternal present. To publish is to find a place in memory.

But to be honest, this entire experience—rupture and rapture—is to a large extent about renewal as a teacher, husband, father, person. There was cleansing involved in it, by which I mean a certain kind of purification that has led me to look at things more simply, without subterfuges. The automatization of modern life is unavoidable, but that doesn't mean we shouldn't resist it.

I now encourage students to toy with words in ways I had never suggested before. And to play with silence. I listen to them with renewed acuteness. Their ideas acquire concrete shapes in my mind. The classroom is a stage, an enormous brain in which all participants are neurons. It is a theater—the theater of knowledge, the theater of memory. And it is a microcosm of the world in which we perform our own lives.

"Everybody who is incapable of learning has taken to teaching," Oscar Wilde said once. I take this maxim at face value. Life is about repetition. But we can't allow that repetition to turn us into automatons. In my case, since teaching felt like an echo chamber, I needed to look elsewhere for answers. Now I know that teaching—e.g., living—must be about showing one's own vulnerabilities. A teacher is someone who enters other people's dreams.

One of my favorite poems is William Butler Yeats's "The Second Coming":

> Turning and turning in the widening gyre
> The falcon cannot hear the falconer;
> Things fall apart; the centre cannot hold;
> Mere anarchy is loosed upon the world,

The blood-dimmed tide is loosed, and everywhere
The ceremony of innocence is drowned;
The best lack all conviction, while the worst
Are full of passionate intensity.

Surely some revelation is at hand;
Surely the Second Coming is at hand.
The Second Coming! Hardly are those words out
When a vast image out of *Spiritus Mundi*
Troubles my sight: somewhere in sands of the desert
A shape with lion body and the head of a man,
A gaze blank and pitiless as the sun,
Is moving its slow thighs, while all about it
Reel shadows of the indignant desert birds.
The darkness drops again; but now I know
That twenty centuries of stony sleep
Were vexed to nightmare by a rocking cradle,
And what rough beast, its hour come round at last,
Slouches towards Bethlehem to be born?

This newness, this reckoning of the soul Yeats describes seldom announces itself beforehand. It just pops up. Which means you'll be taken by surprise. And then what do you do?

Ilan Stavans is Lewis-Sebring Professor of Humanities and Latin American and Latino Culture at Amherst College.

Bill Hughes is a photographer in Montgomery, Massachusetts.